# COOL CARD TRICKS

## Techniques for the Advanced Magician

### Paul Zenon

rosen publishing's
**rosen central**

New York

North American edition first published in 2008 by:

The Rosen Publishing Group, Inc.
29 East 21st Street
New York, NY 10010

North American edition copyright © 2008 by The Rosen Publishing Group, Inc.
First published as *Street Magic* in the United Kingdom, copyright © 2005 by
Carlton Books Limited. Text copyright © 2005 by Paul Zenon. Additional end
matter copyright © 2008 The Rosen Publishing Group, Inc.

North American edition book design: Nelson Sá
North American edition editor: Nicholas Croce
Photography: Karl Adamson (tricks), Rich Hardcastle (remaining images)

**Library of Congress Cataloging-in-Publication Data**

Zenon, Paul.
Cool card tricks: techniques for the advanced magician / Paul Zenon.—North
American ed.
    p. cm.—(Amazing magic)
Contains material previously published in *Street Magic*, © 2005.
Includes bibliographical references and index.
ISBN-13: 978-1-4042-1085-1
ISBN-10: 1-4042-1085-7
1. Card tricks—Juvenile literature. I. Zenon, Paul. Street magic. II. Title. III. Series.
GV1549.Z45 2008
793.8'5—dc22

                                                                        2007010355

*Manufactured in the United States of America*

# CONTENTS

# INTRODUCTION

Do you think of yourself as a cardsharp? In this book you'll tackle more ambitious card tricks. They require a bit more practice but don't worry—you don't need double-jointed fingers or hands quicker than the eye. The techniques described here also can be used to enhance the tricks you'll find in the other books in this series. And you'll get a chance to devise your own routine when you learn the final trick in this book—get those creative juices flowing!

Here we put the icing on the cake when it comes to giving a stunning performance of card magic. Magicians are known for the expert way they can invisibly manipulate a deck, but the special tricks that magicians use to show off their skill are another aspect of card handling. In this book you'll learn how to spread, fan, cut, and shuffle the deck like a professional. There's the added satisfaction of appearing to handle the deck like an expert, even though you know that the trick you're performing almost performs itself!

This is an impromptu demonstration of card manipulation; you take a borrowed, shuffled pack and deal yourself a winning hand of cards. No preparation is needed, but you and your audience will need to have a reasonably advanced understanding of the game of poker.

The first thing you need to be familiar with are the winning hands. They are:

Royal flush: the ten, jack, queen, king, and ace of any suit.
Straight flush: five cards in sequence of the same suit.
Four of a kind: four cards of the same value.
Full house: any three of a kind, plus a pair.
Flush: any five cards of the same suit.
Three of a kind: three cards of the same value.
Two pair: two cards of the same value and two cards of another.

The highest hand is the royal flush and the lowest is two pair, but apart from in the movies, one of the highest hands you'll normally see in a real game is a full house. So anyone who plays poker would be very impressed if you could deal yourself one of those, or even a flush. Never mind four aces. And that's exactly what you do in this trick: you take a shuffled deck of cards and deal yourself a realistic winning hand at poker.

Here's the secret. Don't perform this as a challenge. Just do it casually during a game of cards, or after someone has watched you do a few tricks and asked the inevitable question, "Are you any good at winning at cards?" Ask them to shuffle the cards. "Well, I suppose I could if I wanted. Tell you what; give them a shuffle." Take them back after the shuffle, saying, "If there are any jokers, we need to get rid of them for this; let me just check." Spread through the cards with their faces toward you. You're looking for the jokers, but you're also secretly looking for something else—a good poker hand.

The poker hand you're looking for is any five cards that are already together in the deck and that make up a full house, a flush, or two pair. No matter how much a deck is shuffled, it'll be an unusual and unlucky day if you can't find such a hand.

Now, you need to be paying attention to the cards to make this trick work, and you need to be really familiar with the hierarchy of poker hands; it's easy to miss a winning combination as you quickly run through the cards. It's possible that you might find a great hand that's broken up by one indifferent card—for example, a flush that's got an unwanted card right in the middle. If that's the case, just casually remove it and put it on top of the deck. When and if you find the jokers, take them out, too, and place them on top of the deck. If they've already been removed, no problem; just comment that someone's

already saved you the trouble. You can provide a little additional verbal misdirection as you scan the cards by asking the ambiguous question, "You sure you're playing with a full deck?" The spectator usually will assure you that he is, but the truth is that you might have set a little doubt in his mind; after all, it isn't as if people constantly check whether all the cards are present in a deck.

You need to do one more thing—when you spot a winning hand of cards, crimp the lower left corner of the card immediately to the left of it. Do this by bending it upward with your left thumb (1).

In the photo I've crimped the card immediately above a full house made up of queens and nines.

When you've run through the deck, square it up and take away any jokers you might have found. "OK, the jokers are gone—let's start. Does everyone know how to play poker?" Unless you get a unanimous "no," start your demonstration. "First the cards are cut." You cut your crimp to the bottom, which brings your winning hand to the top. "Then they're dealt, left to right—dealer's is the last hand." Deal out five hands of five cards, dealing to yourself last. Turn over your hand and show which cards you're holding. If it turns out to be a great hand, take all the credit for it and offer to repeat the demonstration. More often than not, it won't be so great. "As you can see—not a lot to play with. Here's where the manipulation comes in." Gather up all the hands, being careful not to alter the position of any of the cards in them. Drop the hands back on top of the deck. Your crimp card is still on the bottom, so you can give the deck several cuts if you feel it might enhance the trick.

The last cut is made at the crimp, sending it back to the bottom. "Let's see what we can do—pay close attention to the right hand." Deal out five hands again and give a running commentary about where the cards are coming from. "I'm dealing regular cards to my opponents . . . all coming off the top of the deck. Watch when I deal my card, though; I'm going to deal myself one from the middle instead. There—did you see it?" Of course they didn't because you took the card off the top just as you did with all the others.

Continue dealing hands and making exaggerated claims when it comes to dealing your own cards. Tell the spectators that they're coming from the middle, bottom, or anywhere else except the top. Name the hand that you spotted earlier; let's say it's a full house.

"Now, it would be foolish to deal myself four aces. If you spot four aces in a hand, you know someone's probably been cheating. So what I'm going for is a full house. You usually can win comfortably with a full house—queens and nines are what I'm looking for." When the deal's finished, turn over your hand. "Queens and nines; let's see what I got." The spectators should be suitably impressed with your hand.

## NOTES

After the deal, I don't bother to show what the other hands of cards are. Luck might have put some very good cards there, and I don't want to spoil my reputation by possibly losing the hand. There's an exception to this rule—if I've managed to find a really spectacular hand, like four of a kind, I'll risk showing all the other hands before revealing my own. And, naturally, in that case I'll take credit for any other interesting hands that are there, claiming that I was deliberately hooking everyone else in before delivering the sucker punch!

In this demonstration you show how easily you can find any four of a kind or royal flush in the deck. Someone selects a card; the ten of hearts, for example. With a snap of the fingers the mate of that card, the ten of diamonds, turns face-up in the middle of the deck. And on the count of three, the remaining pair of tens suddenly appears. That's all four tens, and it took less time to find them than it took to read this paragraph.

This trick makes use of a prearranged stack of cards and a false shuffle. The routine isn't difficult to do, but it looks extremely impressive when performed well. Here's the setup from the top of the deck down: face-down ten of hearts, face-up ten of clubs, face-up ten of spades, and face-up ten of diamonds. The remainder of the deck is face-down underneath these four cards (1).

The first step is to convince your audience that the deck is in random order, and you do that by giving it a false shuffle—one that appears to mix up the cards, but actually brings your stack back to

the top of the deck. Begin with the deck held in the left hand for an overhand shuffle. The right hand cuts the lower half of the deck from underneath and lifts it up. The left thumb pulls off the top card of this right-hand packet, but injogs it in so that it sticks out a little toward you (2). The right hand continues to shuffle cards onto the injogged card, but flush with all the other cards below.

Continue shuffling until there are no more cards in the right hand. The result is that you have a card sticking out toward you, an injog, which lies directly above your setup cards (3). The right hand comes over the deck to give it a cut. The right thumb pulls up on the injogged card, creating a break below it while pushing it in flush with the rest of the top half of the deck (4). The right hand lifts off all the

cards above the break and cuts them to the bottom of the deck. The end result is that although you appear to have given the deck a shuffle and a cut, your prearranged stack is still on top.

You can use this false shuffle in any card routine that requires you to maintain what's known as a "top stock" of cards. You want to create the illusion that you can find any four of a kind in the deck, but in fact, the spectator won't have any option in his apparently free choice; he'll choose the ten of diamonds no matter which card he points to. The cards already are arranged for a very clever "force" devised by magician Henry Christ. You spread the cards from the left hand to the right hand, being careful to keep the top part of the deck bunched together so that the reversed cards can't be seen. Tell one of

the spectators to "point to any one of the cards in the middle. It doesn't matter which one." He does (5).

Break the spread so that the one they point to is the top card of the left-hand packet. Square up the right-hand packet by tapping it against the side of your left hand

and then flip it over and drop it on top of the left-hand packet (6). Spread the cards again as far down as the first face-down card, drawing attention to the face-up cards as you say, "You could have pointed to any one of these cards." Separate the spread so that all the face-up cards are in your right hand. Thumb off the top face-down card of the left-hand packet, saying, "But you chose this one—take a look at it." Because of the ingenuity of Henry Christ's "force," the first face-down card will be the ten of diamonds. Thumb it off the deck so that the spectator can take a look at it (7). I've exposed the reversed ten of hearts in this photo so that you can better understand the position of the setup. It lies third from the top of the left-hand packet, but in actual performance you would be careful not to spread the packet too much or the spectator might spot it.

While the spectator looks at his chosen card, you flip the right-hand packet face-down on top of the left-hand packet and then place the squared-up deck on the table. "This is an old gambler's trick. Let me show you. Which card did you choose? Turn it over." The spectator reveals the ten of diamonds. "OK, ten of diamonds. Let me see if I can remember how to do this. I'm going to try to find the best mate of the ten of diamonds; that'll be the ten of hearts—watch." Snap your fingers over the deck on the table. "It doesn't look like much, does it? But look . . ." Spread the deck to reveal that the ten of hearts is now face-up in the middle (8). Pick up the deck, spread it between your hands, cut the ten of hearts to the top, and place it face-up on the table. "That's two red tens. Let me see if I can find the two black tens." If you've followed the instructions, the two black tens are already on the bottom of the deck.

For the next phase, you need to move one of them to the top of the deck. Here's how you do it. Hold the deck in the left hand in overhand shuffle mode. The right hand cuts half the deck from underneath, but the left fingers contact the bottom/face card of the deck, a black ten,

and hold it in place as the cards above it are removed. The right hand then shuffles its cards onto the left packet. As you reach the last few cards of the right-hand packet, the left thumb peels them off one at a time so that the last card of the packet—one of the black tens— becomes the top card of the deck. You're almost ready for the finale.

Place the deck face-down in the left hand. Both hands are held about eighteen inches apart at waist height. "Watch closely; it'll happen on the count of three." Count "one" and throw the deck from the left hand to the right, which catches it. On the count of "two," throw the deck back to the left hand, except that this time you hold the top and bottom cards back (9). This is easy to do—just press down lightly with the right thumb on the top card of the deck and press upward with the fingers on the bottom card of the deck while giving the hand a sideways jerk to send the rest of the deck flying from between them into the waiting left hand. The top and bottom cards stay in the right hand. Count "three" while turning those two cards face-up and spreading them to show that they're the two black tens (10). All four tens have now made a flashy and surprising appearance.

## NOTES

Obviously you don't have to use the tens in this trick. You could change the story and use the same routine to produce four aces or any other four of a kind.

You also can change the trick slightly to produce different effects. For instance, set the cards up in this order: face-down ace of spades, face-down king of spades, face-down queen of spades, face-down jack of spades, any card face-up, ten of spades face-up, followed by the rest of the deck face-down in any order.

Work the Henry Christ force as described. Because of the arrangement of cards, the spectator will select the ten of spades. Put the right-hand cards on top of the left-hand cards as before, and then place the deck on the table. Ask the spectator to show the card he's chosen, then say, "Ten of spades—not necessarily a great card, but any good card player could make it into a great hand. All they'd have to do is find your ten some good company—like this . . ."

Snap your fingers over the deck and then spread it. There, face-up in the middle of the spread, are the jack, queen, king and ace of spades. Together with his card, they make a royal flush. And you don't get much better than that!

**T**his is a trick that controls the position of a card that depends upon sleight-of-hand, rather than psychology or subtlety. A card is selected, remembered, and replaced in the deck. With just two cuts, you can bring it to the top or bottom of the deck, ready to be produced in any number of ways.

"Take a card," you say in time-honored tradition as you spread the deck from the left hand to the right. "Any one will do—quick as you like." This hurries the spectator along a little. When you're performing, you want to keep the pace up, so act as if you genuinely don't care which card he selects—which in this case happens to be true. "Are you sure?" you ask as soon as the spectator touches a card. Let him take it and then tell him to remember it. "Don't show me; that would make it too easy."

Divide the spread in two at the point from which the card was selected. The spectator remembers the card, shows it around to his friends, and then you extend the left-hand packet saying, "Just drop it

back on top." (1) Don't give him too much time to think about this; just do it, and he'll follow your instructions and place the card back where you want it.

Place the right-hand packet on top of his card, but as you do, secretly keep a break between the packets. To do this, just curl your left little finger around the side and on top of the bottom packet as you drop the top packet onto it (2). The fleshy pad of the little finger prevents the two packets from closing all the way together. From the front, the packets seem to blend together perfectly. You now give the deck two cuts, and in doing so secretly move the selected card to the top of the deck. For this "double undercut," begin by taking the deck from above in the right hand, fingers at the outer short end, thumb at the inner short end. The right thumb takes over the break. The left hand cuts off roughly half of the cards from the lower portion of the deck below the break (3). You can see in the photo how the right thumb maintains the original break as this is done.

The left-hand packet of cards is now placed on top of the deck (4). Then the left hand returns to a position under the deck, takes all the cards below the break, and again places its packet on top of the deck (5). The selected card is now the top card, and in the perfect position for you to reveal it. Performed smoothly, this is a perfectly natural-looking move. It looks as if you've given the deck two quick cuts. You can add to the belief that the selected card has been lost in the deck by giving the cards a false shuffle. To do this, pick up the deck in preparation for an overhand shuffle. Let the upper half of the deck fall from the right hand into the waiting left hand. Now injog the next single card and shuffle the rest of the cards onto the top of that. Square the cards, converting the injog into a break. Cut the cards at the break and complete the cut. The selected card is now on top of the deck.

## NOTES

The same control can be used to position the selected card on the bottom of the deck. When the card is replaced in the deck, it will be jogged slightly over the right side of the bottom packet. The left little finger pushes up on the underside of the card and takes its break underneath it as the right-hand cards are placed on top. The deck is squared up with the selected card above the little finger break. After you make the double undercut, the selected card will be on the bottom of the deck, rather than the top.

There's a saying in magic that if you know one good way to control a chosen card and a hundred ways to reveal it, then you know a hundred tricks. Make the most of that theory.

TRICK 4

"Is this your card?" Unfortunately, the spectator tells you it's not. It appears you've made a bad mistake. Never mind; you take the wrong card and rub it on your sleeve and it magically changes into the right one!

This is achieved by means of a move known as a double lift, which is probably the most used—and sometimes overused—move in card magic. In this example, you'll use it to change one card into another. Let's assume someone's chosen a card and it's been replaced in the deck and apparently lost with a couple of cuts and a shuffle. During this sequence, you've secretly brought the card to the top of the deck using the advanced control.

"You might think that your card's lost in the deck, but I can bring it to the top very quickly—very quickly indeed. All you need to do is say the magic word." Pause a while as if waiting for the spectator to say something and, when he doesn't, repeat with some emphasis the instructions again. "All you need to do is say the magic word."

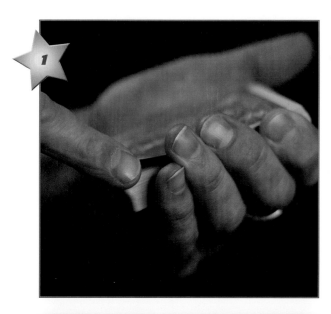

He'll assume that you're joking. Tell him that you aren't—you really do need him to say a magic word! "Any magic word will do. But because you selected the card, it's you who has to say it. Off you go!"

There's fun to be had watching a fully grown adult trying to come up with something that doesn't involve swearing. Let him say his word and then tell him, "No, you've got to say it with a bit more conviction." And make him say it a second time. "That was better that time—and here's your card."

You now appear to turn over the top card, but this is where you perform the double-lift sleight. Instead of turning over the top card, you turn over the top two cards as if they're a single one. With the deck held in the

left-hand dealing grip, the right hand extends its forefinger and pulls up on the cards at the inner end of the deck (1). The fleshy pad of the forefinger catches the top card and drags it upward. Unknown to the spectators, the pad of your finger also contacts a second card and drags it upward, too (2).

Keep pulling upward on the two cards until they close up together. You'll find that if you curl the first joint of the right forefinger inward, the cards will naturally slide together and line themselves up as one. They're held by the right thumb on top and the right forefinger underneath. Drag them both to the side of the deck, holding them there briefly (3).

You can clamp them in place against the top of the deck with the left thumb

and move the right hand away at this point if you want. When you're ready to turn the cards over, grip them again with the right thumb and forefinger at the inner right corner. The left thumb moves out of the way and the right hand flips the two cards face-up onto the deck. The cards hinge over on their long side. This turning action has to be done in one smooth movement, and you should do it so that the two cards land injogged at the inner end of the deck (4).

That's the first part of the move; you've turned over the top two cards together so that they appear to be one single card. Draw attention to the face of the visible card, saying, "And there it is—your card!"

Actually it's the wrong card, and the spectator usually won't waste much time before telling you so. "I knew you weren't really into that magic word business," you reply. You turn the double card back face-down onto the deck. The injog makes this easier. The right hand just takes the two aligned cards at the inner right corner. Drag them to the right of the deck and then flip the pair over (5).

Again the cards hinge on their long side. This time the cards land square on the deck. Thumb off the top card into the right hand. Take it at the inner right corner and rub the face-down card on your left sleeve as if trying to wipe the face off it (6). "It looks like I've got to do all the work round here! What was the name of your card then?" As soon as the spectator has named his selection, use the right third finger to give the card a snap. "That should do it." Turn the card over to reveal that it's now transformed into the chosen card (7).

## NOTES

The double lift is one of the most important moves in card magic. To do it well, you must always remember to handle the two cards as if they really are just one card. At first you'll find it difficult to keep the cards aligned with each other, but it'll become easier with practice. When performed properly, the move is absolutely undetectable. Even professional magicians can't tell whether an expert is actually handling two cards or one. It's even possible to handle three cards as one when you get good!

The key to the move is lightness of touch. Try to appear casual as you flip the cards over onto the deck. As far as the spectators are concerned, you're simply turning over a single playing card—nothing more, nothing less. Too many would-be magicians make the move look like a move!

# TRICK 5

The spectator tries her hand at finding a selected card. You tell her that if she takes a joker and stabs it into the middle of the deck, she'll place that joker right next to the previously chosen card. Funnily enough, she believes you. However, when she tries the trick, she misses. Neither of the cards on either side of the joker proves to be the right one. The surprise comes when she turns over the joker. It's magically changed into the selected card!

"I've been finding your cards all night. It's about time that you did some of the work. Don't worry; it's easy." Use the double lift to turn over the top two cards of the deck as one. Point to the card that's now face-up on top, saying, "Is that your card? No? Good." Name the card—let's assume in this case that it's the joker. Flip the two cards over and thumb the top face-down into the right hand. Be careful not to show its face because this is the selected card. Tell the spectator, "Here's what I want you to do—take the joker, keep it face-down, and stab it somewhere into the middle of the deck. Don't think about it—just do it. Use your intuition and don't worry about being vicious!"

You hand her the face-down card and then hold the deck face-up in the left hand so that she can thrust the card into it at its outer short end (1). She'll stick the card in face-down somewhere in the middle of the deck. Tell her not to let go of the card as you spread the deck from hand to hand (2). Divide the deck at the face-down card. Then ask her whether her chosen card is the top one of the left-hand packet. She'll say no. "So it must be the one on the other side?" Show her the

face card at the bottom of the right spread of cards. Again she'll say no. Look her straight in the eyes, asking, "What card did you choose then?" When she tells you it was the king of hearts, reply, "So what card did you think you were holding?" She'll usually scream when she finds that she's been holding that card all along (3).

## NOTES

This isn't a difficult trick to perform, but it requires good management of the spectator. Don't pick someone who looks as though she might try to spoil the trick by being difficult and maybe taking a premature look at the card in her hand. An alternative, once you've shown the face-up joker after the double lift, is apparently to push it face-down into the deck yourself, square the cards up, and then spread the deck face-up across the table. Push out the face-down card together with the face-up cards on either side of it. When she's denied that either of the face-up cards is hers, ask her to turn over the face-down card. She'll be amazed.

**T**his is classic magic in which the spectator's selected card rises to the top of the deck again and again and again, even when the cards are in his own hands.

This trick is a standard, and most magicians have their own favorite version. I'll break the trick down into different stages so that you can learn each phase separately and then combine them together in any way that suits you.

## The First Rise

Spread the cards face-down between your hands and ask a spectator to choose one. As he takes it, separate the deck at that point and square up both halves. He looks at, remembers, and then replaces his card on top of the lower left-hand pile. You shuffle off a single card from the right-hand pile onto the top of the left, injogging it as in the advanced control method, then shuffle the rest of the right-hand cards on top of that. Now, rather than pushing up with the right thumb to make the break below the injogged card, you push down to make the break above it. Continue with the double undercut. This time the selected card has ended up second from the top. "This isn't one of those tricks in which you take a card and I tell you what it is. In this trick, you take a card and you tell me what it is. No, really; what was your card?" When the spectator announces the name of his card—let's say it's the jack of clubs, you say, "I don't believe it! The jack of clubs? That's the most ruthlessly ambitious card in the deck. It's never happy unless it's on top. Look . . ."

Flip over the top card of the deck in the same way that you'd do a double lift, and then flip it face-down again as you say, "It's not here." Flip the entire deck over in the left hand, displaying the bottom/face card while saying, "And it's not here." Turn the deck face-down again. "But if I snap my fingers, watch what happens." Snap your right finger and thumb, and then do a double lift. The jack of clubs now appears as if it's the top card of the deck.

## The Second Rise

"I'll do that again," you say. "The first time's always too fast." Flip the double card face-down onto the deck. Thumb off the top card as though it's the jack you just displayed and take it in the right hand. Insert it into the deck from the inner short end (1). Push the card flush. "The jack goes into the middle, but if I snap my fingers, it claws its way right back to the top of the pile again." Turn over the top card to show that the jack's back.

## The Third Rise

This sequence uses a move called Tilt, invented by the late Ed Marlo, a Chicago card expert. At the moment, the jack is still face-up on top of the deck. Flip it face-down and thumb it off into the right hand. As you're about to put the jack into the middle of the deck as you did before, you show its face one more time. Your right hand raises the card so that the spectators are now in no doubt that you are actually holding the jack of clubs (2).

"Watch jack jump." As the spectators look at the jack, the left hand prepares for the tilt move. Lower the left hand toward you and push the top card over a little with your thumb. Pull it back again, but retain a break below it with your little finger. Move the left thumb so that it lies along the left side of the deck. This will allow the top card to pop up into the tilt position; this is one in which a large break is held between the inner end of the top card and the rest of the deck.

Always keep the right side of the deck turned away from the audience. If you keep the surface of the top card parallel with the floor, the spectators won't suspect the gap at the rear of the deck. It takes skill to learn to set up the tilt position with one hand, but once mastered it only

5

takes a moment and the showing of the jack provides all the cover you need. Hold the deck just below chest height. The right hand lowers the jack and appears to push it into the middle of the deck as before, but really pushes it into the gap and along the top of the main portion of the deck (3 and 4).

From the spectator's point of view the jack appears to be going into the middle of the deck, but really it ends up second from the top. Push the jack flush with the rest of the deck, then give it a shake and, as you do so, allow the break between the deck and the top card to collapse. Snap your fingers and then make a double lift, turning the top two cards over as one to reveal that the jack seems to have somehow climbed back to the top again.

## Final Rise

Flip the double card face-down and thumb the top one off into the right hand. "Maybe you'll see how it works if I use fewer cards. Just cut some off and leave me about half the deck." The spectator believes you've got the jack face-down in the right hand. He reaches over to the deck and cuts off half of the cards (5).

You now insert the right-hand card into the middle of the cards you're holding in the left hand (6). Make it look exactly the same as your previous handling. "OK, there are not many cards here. Watch jack jump back to the top again." Snap your fingers and then proudly flip over the top card of the packet. The jack isn't there. Act surprised. "Hmm. Maybe he went to the bottom, then . . ." Flip the

packet over. No jack there either. Spread the cards face-up between the hands as if searching for the jack. "Wait a minute—I know what happened. He didn't jump to the top of my cards; he jumped to the top of yours!" Ask the spectator to turn over the top card of the packet he's holding. "There you go!" (7).

## NOTES

If you want to elaborate on the routine, you can add more phases by using some of the tricks and moves you've already learned. For instance, perform the routine as a way of finding a chosen card in the conventional way. The spectator looks at his card, replaces it in the deck, and you use a credit card to find it. Then you tell him that not only is the card radioactive, but it also can perform a quantum leap in the deck. You shuffle his card into the deck as you talk, but in fact you use a false shuffle to bring the card to the second position from the top of the deck and then perform the First Rise phase of this routine.

Or use a handling of Trick 5 as follows: Let's imagine that you've secretly brought the selected card, the jack of clubs, to the top of the deck. Do a double lift to show that the top card isn't the one you're looking for. Turn the double card face-down, thumb it off, and hand it to the spectator, saying, "But if you wave that card over the deck, the jack will appear on the top."

The spectator waves the card he's holding, and then you turn over the top card of the deck. It still isn't the jack. Flip the deck over, saying, "Maybe it went to the bottom, then." It isn't there either. Spread the face-up cards as if looking for the missing jack of clubs. Then, as if an idea's suddenly dawned on you, turn to the spectator and say, "I know what happened; the jack jumped too far—look!" He'll be amazed to find that he's actually holding onto the jumping jack.

This trick is a showstopper of a routine, and the more you know about card magic, the more you can personalize this trick and devise a routine that's unique to you.

# TRICK 7

The benchmark of a good card manipulator is to be able to spread the deck in an even fan so that the numbers of all the cards are showing. Here's how you can add this impressive trick to your card work.

The advantage of the pressure fan above other fanning techniques is that it works with most types of playing cards. If you're really interested in card magic, then avoid really cheap decks of cards and, equally, expensive-looking cards that have been plastic-coated. The best cards are the type used in casinos; they wear well and don't grow thick and dog-eared with use.

To make a pressure fan, start with the deck in the right hand, with the thumb at the inner short end and the fingers at the outer short end. Hold out the left hand and press the lower part of the deck against the left fingers (1). You're now going to fan the deck in a clockwise direction. To do this, bend the deck between the right fingers

and thumb. Now move the right hand in a clockwise direction with the right thumb acting as a pivot for the action. As the right hand moves, it allows the cards to spring, under pressure, from the right hand and onto the left. They're left behind gradually in a neat arc as the right hand moves. The left thumb is kept out of the way. At this

point it's only the firm presence of the right hand that prevents the cards from falling to the floor. When the right hand has reached the lowest point of its arc, the left thumb clamps the deck to the left hand (2).

The right hand now can move away and you should be left with a perfect fan. From the front, the indices of virtually all the cards should be visible (3). To close the fan, the right forefinger contacts the lower-right edge of the fan and pushes it back in an anti-clockwise direction until all the cards are squared in the left hand.

## NOTES

The pressure fan looks flashy. It's designed to impress the spectators, but as with all the tricks in this book, you should be careful how you use it. It shows that you're familiar and comfortable with the deck, but if you overuse moves like this one, you risk being looked upon as a show-off. Sometimes tricks can make a routine look elegant, but at other times they can actually detract from the magic. They make the tricks look as if they're purely the result of manual dexterity, rather than something more esoteric. In fact, there are magicians who deliberately fake being clumsy with the cards so their audiences don't believe their tricks could result purely from sleight-of-hand and, therefore, their magic seems all the more mysterious. It's basically a judgment call, but a really important one, and you should seriously consider what fits your own personal style and the kind of impression you want to leave your audience with.

TRICK 8

This is the classic attention-getting magician's trick—spraying the cards noisily over a distance from one hand to the other. It isn't easy; it takes practice. But you will feel cool when you can do it!

I'm left-handed. And because most of the readers of this book will be right-handed, I had to learn to do all the tricks in this book the right-handed way. Otherwise, the photographs wouldn't have made much sense. Well, there's one trick I still can't do right-handed, and it's this one. So I hope you'll indulge me because what follows is a description of how I perform this trick.

You right-handers will have to reverse the left/right instructions to learn the trick. Now you see what I've had to put up with for all these years! I'm going to start with the deck held in the left hand, fingers on the outer short end and thumb on the inner short end, and then spring the cards from the left hand into the waiting right

hand. I'm also putting pressure on the cards by squeezing the thumb and fingers together. You can see the cards starting to bend in the photo (1).

With the left hand palm-down so that the cards are about nine or so inches above the right hand, I then apply more pressure to the

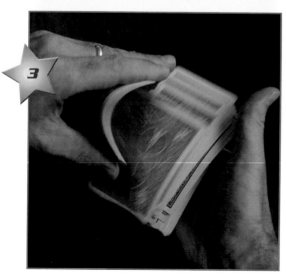

cards, squeezing the left fingers and thumb together. If you do this correctly, you'll find that you can allow the cards to squirt free of the left hand. They slip off the left thumb and shoot in a continuous and unbroken stream to be caught in the right hand (2).

There's a skill to this, particularly in allowing the cards to slip off the thumb, rather than both the fingers and the thumb, which will usually just result in them spraying all over the place. Once you've mastered it, you can increase the distance between your hands by moving the top hand higher. Also, try holding the right hand close the body and the left hand a little farther away. You then spring the card toward the body and the right hand. You can use your body as a barrier to stop the cards bouncing out of the right hand and falling to the floor. You also might find it useful to bring your hands back closer together as the last of the cards leave the left hand (3).

One distinctive characteristic of this trick is the cool sound of the cards squirting out of your hand one after the other—do this trick in a bar and you'll soon have everyone's attention.

## NOTES

Before trying to squirt the cards over too great a distance, first concentrate on mastering the release of the cards from the left hand. Try to make the springing of the cards controlled and even—it's not a quick burst of flying cards that you're trying to achieve; it's a longer, steady stream.

Although I let the cards escape from the thumb of my left hand, many other magicians prefer to let the cards escape from their fingers and spring from the hand in a forward motion. It's purely a matter of personal preference.

With practice, you'll find that you can hold your hands farther and farther apart. You can play with variations; for example, beginning with the hands close together, start to spring the cards and then move them apart so that the river of cards gets larger and then; just as the last of the cards has left your hand, bring your hands quickly back together, square the deck, and you're ready to begin your performance.

This is how gamblers shuffle cards. They split the deck into two and riffle the halves together, finishing it off with a fancy "waterfall" trick. Master this shuffle and you look like you really know what you're doing with a deck.

The riffle shuffle can be used to great effect. Start with the deck, held vertically in the left hand. The lower short end of the deck rests on the curled fingers, the thumb is on the top end of the deck, and the cards are facing toward your right. Holding back the top half of the deck with the left thumb at the upper end (1), allow the bottom half of the deck to fall onto the waiting right fingers (2). Push upward on the bottom end of the bottom packet with the left fingers, pivoting it on the right fingers so that it flips over and up with the right thumb taking hold of it so that it's in exactly the same grip as the left-hand packet (3).

The fingers of each hand hold the lower part of the packets. You'll find that if you curl the fingers tightly under the cards, you'll

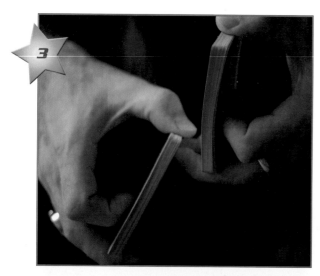

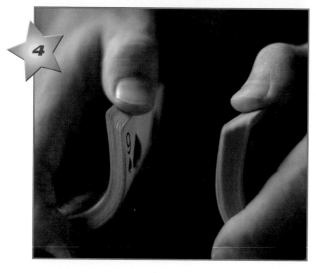

get a good firm grip. At the same time, the thumbs pull back on the upper end of the packets, bending them backward in preparation for the shuffle (4).

To shuffle the packets together, turn them toward a horizontal position and allow the inner ends to simultaneously slip free of the thumbs in a riffling action (5). The two packets interlace. Keep riffling the cards together as evenly as you can until both thumbs have no cards left. At this stage you could push the two halves together to reform the deck; however, there's an additional and even more fancy finish to the shuffle called the "waterfall."

To do the waterfall, you flex the cards upward into an arch by pressing inward and up with your curled fingers. The thumbs press down on top of the arch to stop the cards unweaving (6). At this point the cards are under quite a lot of pressure. If you now gradually relax your fingers downward and outward, the cards will cascade down and fall together with an impressive rushing

5

6

sound (7). When all the cards have fallen, just push the cards together and square up the deck.

## NOTES

This is a very professional-looking shuffle and immediately marks you as someone who is familiar with cards and card play. Although it appears that the shuffle mixes the cards thoroughly, you can include an element of card control very easily.

Let's imagine you know the selected card is on top of the deck. You want to shuffle the cards, but you don't want to lose track of it. All you do is allow the top card to fall last during the shuffle. If you've followed the instructions, the selected card will be on top of the left-hand packet. When you riffle the cards together, riffle the left-hand packet more slowly, allowing its top card to fall last. This ensures that the top card of the deck will remain on top, even after the shuffle.

Two quick riffle shuffles in succession should convince anyone you've thoroughly mixed the deck, but leaves you in a position to perform whichever particular revelation of his card you care to.

**H**ere's another fancy way of manipulating the deck that gives the impression of great manual dexterity. In this trick, you hold the deck up and give it a one-handed cut. No one's going to want to play poker with you once they've seen you do this.

The one-handed cut is sometimes known as the Charlier Cut, named after a nineteenth-century card manipulator. There's no doubt that Charlier was an outstanding card manipulator, but there's no real evidence that he invented this particular method of cutting the cards. For whatever reason, however, the name seems to have stuck. You can use either hand to perform the move; let's describe this one for the lefties again.

Hold the deck face-down between the fingers on one long side and the thumb on the other. You'll notice that the left forefinger is curled below the deck (1). The thumb now relaxes pressure on its side of the deck and allows a break to open up, splitting the deck roughly in two (2).

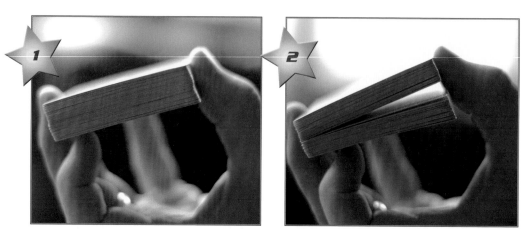

Let this lower portion of the deck fall away from the thumb, hinging at the fingers side, to drop onto the palm. Its fall is controlled by the forefinger underneath, which then pushes the far side of the lower packet upward toward the thumb. The forefinger continues to push it up toward you until it clears the edge of the upper packet (3). This results in the upper packet dropping onto the back of your forefinger. Uncurl the left forefinger from beneath the deck, allowing what was the upper packet to drop onto your palm, then push down with the left thumb on top of the other packet, snapping the halves of the deck together (4).

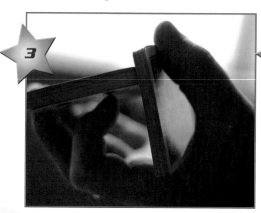

If you now curl the forefinger back under the cards, you will find that you can push the entire deck back up to its original position between the thumb and fingers (5). That's it—you've cut the deck and completed the cut with one hand in no more than a second. If you're feeling really flashy, why not practice it with both hands and then do it using half the deck in each simultaneously? (6). The one-handed cut can be used in any routine that uses a key card. Cutting the deck repeatedly looks as if you're mixing up the cards, but in fact the cuts do nothing to separate your key card from the spectator's selection.

## NOTES

As mentioned earlier, tricks are great for displaying your dexterity, but they can detract from the magic. They also can make it look as if you're showing off; after all, you are! An occasional one can be used to great effect, though, especially in gambling routines where you're apparently demonstrating the grifter's tricks of the trade. It's perfectly legitimate to perform one of these fancy cuts if you're talking about seeing a gambler or card cheat doing it. In this case the trick illustrates how clever the cheat was, and it looks a lot less like you're just trying to be flashy.

T his is a great, eye-popping climax to any trick where you discover a chosen card. You give the cards a simple cut and, as the halves of the deck are placed together, the selected card suddenly shoots out across the table.

This is a simple method for a showy revelation. Ideally, it should be performed on a smooth, polished table, the slick surface allowing the card to spin across it much farther than a cloth-covered surface would. Let's assume that a card's been selected and replaced, and you've controlled it to the bottom of the deck by means of a crimp. The right hand holds the deck with the thumb on the inner long edge and the fingers on the outer long edge, and the left hand adjusts to a similar grip, but underneath the deck. The left little finger curls in and contacts the face of the selected card. From this position, it's easy for it to press on the face of the bottom card and push it to the right so that it projects for about an inch (1).

The right fingers hide the projecting card from the spectators. The right hand holds the deck as the left hand lets go, turns over, and cuts off

a portion of cards from the top of the deck, carrying them forward and placing them on the table (2). The right hand now moves forward as if to place its packet on top of the one on the table. But as it does, the right third finger starts to pull back on the pro-jecting card, putting it under pressure (3).

Just before you place the right packet on top of the packet on the table, allow the bottom card to spring forward off the right third finger (4). It'll shoot and spin a considerable way across the table.

## NOTES

This is a really surprising move; it's totally unexpected when the card pops out of the deck and shoots toward the spectators. It makes an impressive, flashy finish to any trick in which you are producing four of a kind; say, aces; just control the last ace to the bottom of the deck and have it propel itself across the table as you give the cards a cut.

# GLOSSARY

**advanced control**  The act of bringing a card to the top of the deck. A card is selected, remembered, and then replaced in the deck. With just two cuts, you can bring it to the top or bottom of the deck, ready to be produced in any number of ways.

**Charlier Cut**  Named after a card professional of the nineteenth century, the Charlier Cut is the process of cutting a deck of cards using only one hand.

**deal**  To take the cards, one at a time from the top of the deck and place them on the table. The cards can be dealt in a pile on the table. In a card game, the cards would be dealt around the table, going to each player's hand in clockwise rotation.

**deck**  Another name for a pack of cards. Magicians usually use the term deck when talking card tricks.

**double lift**  This is a trick in which two cards are lifted as though they are one and turned over on top of the deck. It can be used to change one card into another.

**false shuffle**  A shuffle that controls the position of some or all of the cards in the deck. You might have a key card on the bottom of the deck. A false shuffle apparently mixes the cards up, but, in fact, the key card is still at the bottom of the deck.

**grifter**  A slang term for a con artist.

**injog**  When a card protrudes out of the pack toward the performer, it's said to be injogged.

**key card**  A key card is a known card that indicates the position of a spectator's selected card. For instance, you might know that the ace of spades is the bottom card of the deck. During the trick, you contrive to get the ace of spades right next to the spectator's chosen card. You now know that whatever card is next to the ace of spades is the selection.

**misdirection**  This is redirecting the audience's attention to something other than the method of the trick. For example, you might gaze at the left hand during a trick to encourage the audience to believe that a coin is there. Looking in the direction of the left hand discourages the audience from looking at the right hand, where the coin actually is palmed.

**revelation**  Magicians talk about the revelation at the end of a trick. This might be the discovery or naming of a selected card or the revealing of a prediction. It denotes the finale.

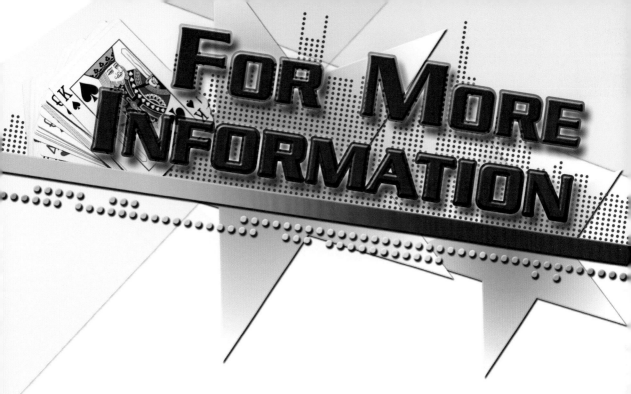

# For More Information

Dr. Bob's Magic Shop
82867 Miles Avenue
Indio, CA 92201
(760) 342-3044
Web site: http://www.magicstor.com

The Magic Castle
Academy of Magical Arts
7001 Franklin Avenue
Hollywood, CA 90028-8600
(323) 851-3313
Web site: http://www.magiccastle.com

The Magic Depot!
7914 East 40th Street
Tulsa, OK 74145
(918) 641-0707
Web site: http://www.magic.org

Magic Hut
433 Lincoln Road
Miami Beach, FL 33139
(888) 42 MAGIC (426-2442)
E-mail: info@magichut.net
Web site: http://www.magichut.net

Magic Web Channel
P.O. Box 81391
Las Vegas, NV 89180
(702) 376-4727
Web site: http://www.magicwebchannel.com

## Web Sites

Due to the changing nature of Internet links, Rosen Publishing has developed an online list of Web sites related to the subject of this book. This site is updated regularly. Please use this link to access the list:

http://www.rosenlinks.com/am/cctr

# FOR FURTHER READING

Angel, Criss. *Mindfreak: Secret Revelations*. New York, NY: HarperEntertainment, 2007.

Copperfield, David. *David Copperfield's Beyond Imagination*. New York, NY: HarperCollins Publishers, 1997.

Frost-Sharratt, Cara. *101 Clever Card Tricks*. London, England: Hamlyn, 2006.

Ho, Oliver. *Young Magician: Card Tricks* (Young Magician). New York, NY: Sterling Publishing Co., 2005.

Hugard, Jean. *Encylopaedia of Card Tricks*. Slough, England: Foulsham, 2003.

Lemezma, Marc. *Mind Magic: Extraordinary Tricks to Mystify, Baffle and Entertain*. London, England: New Holland, 2005.

Longe, Bob. *Giant Book of Card Tricks*. New York, NY: Sterling Publishing Co., 2003.

Schiffman, Nathaniel. *Abracadabra!: Secret Methods Magicians & Others Use to Deceive Their Audience*. Amherst, NY: Prometheus Books, 1997.

# INDEX

## About the Author

Paul Zenon has dozens of TV credits to his name, including his own shows *Paul Zenon's Trick or Treat*, *Paul Zenon's Tricky Christmas*, and *White Magic with Paul Zenon*. He also has appeared on many other television shows, including *History of Magic, Secret History—Magic at War, The World's 50 Greatest Magic Tricks*, and many more. Zenon has performed in around thirty countries and in every conceivable location, from the Tropicana Hotel in Las Vegas to the hold of an aircraft carrier in the Adriatic; from the London Palladium to a clearing in the jungles of Belize; from the Magic Castle in Hollywood to the back of a truck in the Bosnian war zone.

**Designers:** Interior, Nelson Sá; Cover, Tahara Anderson
**Editor:** Nicholas Croce
**Photography:** Karl Adamson